# The Needle In My Veins

## Euridyce J

notionpress
.com

INDIA · SINGAPORE · MALAYSIA

ISBN  979-8-89446-994-2

This book has been published with all efforts taken to make the material error-free after the consent of the author. However, the author and the publisher do not assume and hereby disclaim any liability to any party for any loss, damage, or disruption caused by errors or omissions, whether such errors or omissions result from negligence, accident, or any other cause.

While every effort has been made to avoid any mistake or omission, this publication is being sold on the condition and understanding that neither the author nor the publishers or printers would be liable in any manner to any person by reason of any mistake or omission in this publication or for any action taken or omitted to be taken or advice rendered or accepted on the basis of this work. For any defect in printing or binding the publishers will be liable only to replace the defective copy by another copy of this work then available.

And medicine, law, business, engineering, these are noble pursuits and necessary to sustain life. But poetry, beauty, romance, love, these are what we stay alive for.

— **Dead Poets Society** —

# Acknowledgement

I'm not exactly an established enough author so it feels ridiculous to be congratulating and thanking people.

But this is to acknowledge my support system through this entire process.

Thank you, mom and dad, for being my biggest cheerleader, for being more excited for me than I ever am, for being sadder at my situations than I ever am.

Everyone knows it but I'll say it just in case, I'd be nothing without you.

The three friends that I call my family, Gandhi, Aditi, Bhavya and Gandhi again, I wouldn't even have thought of doing this and sure wouldn't have come this far without you three. This is as much your book as its mine.

And to my melancholy muse, about who most of the poems are about.

And lastly thanks to these poems, which are basically an outlet for my emotions when they're too hard to handle.

*THANK YOU*

# Preface

"When you reach my core at the end
With nothing left of me to defend
Will you look back and wonder too?
If my soul was weak or it just belonged to you"


What happens when the pain you thought would pass,
doesn't?
What happens when you realise it's not just a thing of
youth?
Who do you blame for it?
The ones who couldn't see it?
The ones who saw and did nothing?
The ones who tried to help but gave up?
Or the ones who never tried at all?
And what if all of them is the same person?
Writing poems instead of fixing herself?

# Index

# Unspoken Duels

If you ask me to, I can pinpoint
The exact moment it all started going wrong
The wrong tone of voice
The right strike of words
Forgetting but never forgiving the fights
Stinging stories and the playful bites

I'll never tell you where it hit
When you threw the axe with all your strength
To have you caress the wound gently
Just to do it all over again

I'll never tell you why it hurt
Which nerve did you strike this time
For when the next duel occurs
I won't have it in my spine

To reopen the wound one last time
And try to garner the strength below
To make an armour against your spears
And find it shattered ages ago

My unhealed scars covered by paper
Wouldn't as much protect a hair
When you slice through the skin bit by bit
Reach the bones and find them bare
When you reach my core at the end
With nothing left of me to defend
Will you look back and wonder too?
If my soul was weak or it just belonged to you

# The Doomed War

And we'll have another battle
When you so much feel the hint of a blow
The venom dripping from my mouth
And your ammunition that I helped grow

The blood splashing all over the sink
With each plunge of the dagger
For neither of us will back down
Until we've bled each other dry

My war cry that went unanswered
You winning flag when I scream murder
Your silent sobs that I denounce
As my victorious knife rests for once

Is this payment or just a tragedy
Who explains this broken reality
A narrator or just a cruel
Artist drawing a crimson pool

Of blood that no one will see
Except the ones who dance in glee
In a circle with no end
While I display my wounds and you pretend

You bury them alive and I decide
To showcase them over a worthy prize
The winner gets a heartfelt word
For considering my feelings just above dirt

# You and Me

I read about something called Dracunculus
It's such a beautiful parasite to aggravate
It preys on your blood, penetrates your skin
And quite literally takes your breath away

But who is to say? What his intentions really were?
Why he tore through the skin and the nerves below
Maybe he was just looking for a vein astray
Maybe all he wanted was a companion who would stay

It must really love its host
It leaves its ashes here and there
As memories of their time well spent
That turn to a blister blue and grey

But the moulds it creates on the skin
With his own mouth and toxins from it

All rupture with a single flick of water
Doused under a fuming stream
It would leave the diseased to never return
If only the host remembered how to reach the sea


You can see its gentle touch of regret
Another ironic epiphany
After it tears the muscles it so loved once
I was reminded of you and me

# Imposter Among the Brave

The comfort in his harsher tones
The lullaby of my breaking bones
The tranquil touch of flying stones
And my splintered heart that he owns

The sedation of his whispered lies
The thrill of the emotional highs
My tears hidden in a weak disguise
With my smile as it shrivels and dies

And there it is, my Achilles heel
The delight in his eyes as I kneel
Before his pride and the dark appeal
And the sick heart that I conceal

And what for does my mind wait
Dangling, shredding, in a rotten state
Looking for fantasies to relate
From his words and the holes they create

It would be cruel to enslave
An imposter among the brave
Who'd die trying to become something you crave
And scribble your thorns all over her grav

# Mom....

Would my silence be the final straw?
If I stitch my lips with threads of your words
If I gulp down the blood filling my mouth
Will you finally see my pain
Will you finally understand?

Will you see how your words strike?
Will you finally see the fault of your tone aknew
Will you finally see the monster you created
That is an exact clone of you

Or maybe I should strike back
Spit out the poison instead of trying to gulp it down
After all the venom that threatens to spill from my mouth
Was also birthed by you

Your womb created my limbs and teeth
And your words created my tears and screams
And no one can hear them wash ashore
Not even my own ears believe them anymore

They say it's all my fault no one loves me
And it says it in your voice

I'm undeserving of the love I receive
How could this be untrue?
How could I not believe every single word
After all it was said by the mother who loved me too

Why did I not inherit?
Your stone like eyes unwilling to see
My cry for help and struggling chokes
Or anything past your own agony

My lips are jarred and I've lost my voice
Screaming at an immovable wall
As it laughs at my emotions and pities me
I got your rage and I got your venom
But I didn't get your lack of empathy

Why do you look so surprised when I show you
just how deep the wounds go?
Just how distorted my face becomes
When I try to see myself as anything but you


You seem shocked mother?
Watching my face contort to a demon
To give back the same unstable mixture of love and threats
That was handed to me as a child beaten


Why do you look so surprised?
Watching my teeth sharp and pointed
Ready to rip out throats and veins
Afterall I borrowed your axe to sharpen it


How is it my borrowed pain from your past
Is named an origin unclean?
How is it I'm blamed for leaving red handprints
but my bleeding arms remain unseen?


The new parts of me that you stitched on
Would tear me if I ripped them out
But don't you ever worry mother
Of me trying to find peace elsewhere too
unlike the childhood that was supposed to be mine
Your Frankenstein won't abandon you

How horrifying would that day be
When I look at a mirror and realize that
all the people that i scratched and clawed
And all the lives my sword claimed
All saw the same phantom before their death
That I witnessed when you hailed above me


So go ahead and hide behind your facade and cruel laughs
Stop yourself before you see your crimes
Block your eardrums with my skin
Before you hear the painted whines


What's sadder is the crack in my voice
The helpless sound that comes out of it
Unable to scream out my anger from my lungs
Unable to blame the entity that created it


So if you feel like you won
When you see me cry hearing your words
You would be entirely correct
In assuming my weakness up aboard


And so the next time when we fight
Go ahead and remind me of my weak statue
Numb me to my own emotions
Until I stop loving you too

I did all the same things in my life
Blocked my ears to chants that rang true
About my killing spree and tainted lives
That suffered from both me and you
And I can't even hate you for it
Treat you as the monster you are
Because behind this hideous green and grey cloak
Is the woman that fed me her heart

And I keep getting phantom visions of her
And my return into her arms
Knowing she's long gone doesn't do much
to remove the memory of her wealthy warmth

So even if you decide to tear me next
For your newest collection of gowns
If you're needle finds my eyes to be a welcome home
I won't hold it against you mom

I'll keep on hounding from beneath the wall
Right until my knuckles bleed
I'll keep on hounding the armour
Even though its neither my war nor my country

# Dear Brother

How do your turn your eyes?
To my drowning cries
To my thrashing limbs
Trying to loosen the rope around my neck
To vomit the water out my lungs
All you manage to see is a girl who doesn't deserve what
she received

Do you think I was born with it?
This forked tongue and black coated teeth
Don't you think there was someone behind the curtains
Pulling my veins with invisible strings

Why do you see me with those cruel eyes
My muddy wounds as my own make?
How do you hate me so for carrying a knife
When I only learned how to strike back

I only learnt how to defend my chest
From a blacksmith way too eager
Welding the sharpest needle known to man
Impaling me with all the same with it


Don't you think I was a child too?
Don't you think I deserved the same sympathy?
That you handed out like welfare gifts
To everyone who was not me


How do you manage to be blind?
When it comes to my dark lessons
When I was being taught how to use
My sentences as a taught weapon


But no.
All you could see was the new attire
The shining dark and gold snake
Never mind my hidden scars painted
beneath
Or what was stitched to make it


Oh yes how could I forget
You realize the actual issue
childish pleas of help and the problems created by a fool
I paint myself maroon for pleasure
And then I point to you

# Nothing to Hate
# You For

I had it pretty good, didn't I?
Before I took it all for granted
The sweet kisses whispering over the graveyards
And over the trees that it haunted

I decided to chase the thrill instead
Momentarily though, it chased me too
The storm bearing my name went through me
Before it ever happened to you

So, I decided to make you the villain of my story
With my loved ones cheering through the door
And I sit and wonder how they loathe you so
And I have nothing to hate you for

# The Tale of a Bitter Legacy

The father never experienced love
So don't expect him to show you any
He wanted his children to have everything he didn't
Except for the warmth, peace and penny

The mother learnt cruelty early on
How the relations you know can twist and stab
She faced the demons and broke before their blade
So the poison she heard slipped before she realized
in the homemade food she made

But how can you hate them for being unloved?
And how can you not when you were too?
how can you blame them for what they never felt?
And how can you not when you never felt it too?

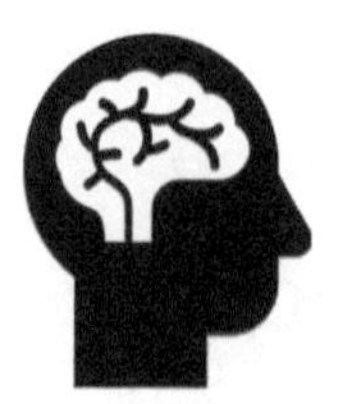

# Lack of Validation

I'm scared to become the next patient
Suffering from lack of validation
The wards would be full of me waiting
To surgically remove an illness so ancient

Scared to lose those too
Who came along as I used them to heal
Because I knew they wouldn't peak inside
For as long as l asked for a veil

But somewhere inside they would be tired
With me being so needing
Their own lives put on hold
For the insecurities I keep on feeding

And then they'd watch me play victim
Like I had the universe's weight
That pulled me down under the surface
As I wrote my own fate

The advices that made my footing
And the warnings that I didn't heed Tired of being my
emotions guardian
And of the crutch that I shouldn't even need


Before I realize they would see me
for who I am, Watch as I strangle the broken plea
Wrap the threads around my throat, while I'm
Webbing schemes to make them love me
Forcing them to hype me up
Give the words with a spoon and a cup
Feed me words like an infant
While I find happiness to corrupt


For how long will they be able?
To play the part of a parent stable
Trying to fill the bottomless hole
Teach me to fight while rocking the cradle

To them I might become a chore
Forcing them to empathize
And listen to my heart that I pour
In All my poems that you adore

No one else wants to listen
To my lamenting stories gleam
And then you come and beg for a line
In the lore of my sleepless dream

So they become about you
And how you make my heart full
All it does is agonize over us
And then it beats for you

No one else really wants to peak
Inside to see the ugly brute
But you care for it like a mother
And it relates to you

Days become the numbers on the clock
To wait for your next word
Time is counted by your smiles
And all the lines that it blurred.

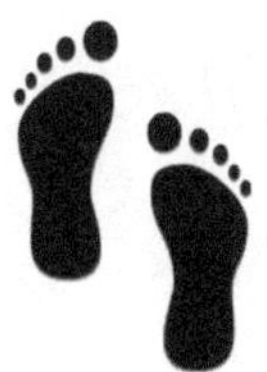

# The Dirt on My Feet

My insecurities they
Leave a muddy footprint

Over the map of our lives I create
Wars spanning hundreds of decades

Spent in a single moment of glance
As the arrows shot from my hand
Reach their mark and never return

For the ashes of our bond I hold,
To sprinkle over the pyres I burn

I grieve the death of the boy I loved
And I grieve over the boy I killed

# Queen Midas of Ashes

What could an empty can of shell
Possibly be happy with?
As she sets ablaze all she can see
So the ashes are stuffed in her chest
Right where the heart was supposed to be

She walks the night with her black gown
Goes until the light is shed
Until she owns every papercut
Until she's the monster under your bed

Her cape as dark as the night
Slithers behind at the wake of joy
It drags on the ground as she walks ahead
Along with the other fools who fell

For the shiny cover of tin they saw
That shined among the hidden gems

She steals their joy and she steals their heart
And stuffs it in her dress like a glutton
She scrambles searching like an infant later
As they vanish in her blue night gown

No matter how many smiles she takes
She can never produce her own
She mirrors the harvest done by another
With every broken reflection of her
Whoever she touches turns to nothing
Their organs decorate her crown atop
A dead lamb would never suffice
For queen Midas of the ashes

What would bring her joy today?
Having your heart in her fist?
Or clenching until it drains again?
Having another beauty, she can mangle with her bare
hands?

I speak to her with a whispered voice
When I stare at a lake and stars made new
I tell her gently about my crimes
I ask her why I murdered you?

Was I trying to fill an empty shell?
With your adoring eyes and your broken smile?
The way you worshipped me was just enough
To distract me from my hollow chest

You pulled me from her arms that day
As I was hanging from a golden thread
Your joy and wrath, and cries and warmth
That reeked of human innocence

Or maybe it's a companion I craved
Someone to rule the darkness with
Someone who would know my heart
And someone just as empty

I can't find and so I make
A slave to my journey awake
A willing doll chained to my pain
Never realizing the actual villain

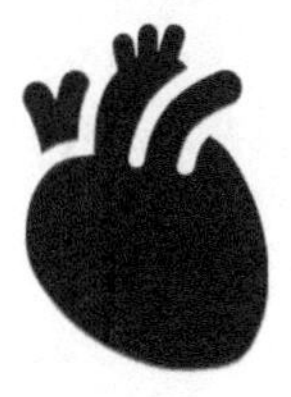

# It

Break it into a million little pieces if you must
If that's how you want them to decorate your highs
A whip would probably not suffice for the agony it
deserves
It longs to be strangled by your sweet lies


Its tiny, moronic and doe eyed staring at you
Drain it of everything it has with your bare hands
So at least your skin recognises the beat my heart sang
to you


Warped in a blacker infinity I'm clutching to my dignity
tooth and nail
The last shred of myself I recognise
I sit woven into the ground by the words you said
My esteem hangs from my fingers as i let it rip
It was yours to tear anyway

# Would it Be Too Selfish?

Is it too selfish to ask you?
To let me scratch that old wound one more time
Just another hit.
Just one more time
For my satisfaction
Till I'm sated and drunk on your words stay here
And then you can leave when with the wounds and a blunt
spear

Just one more time,
Say my name and something mean
So my heart can beat just as fast as this
Because waiting for your voice
As harsh as it maybe
Is the only time I feel something

However sick my heart maybe
From Between the white gowns you love to chase it so
When I run from your claws
It waits for me to stop and turn Look for someone I used
to know

It waits for the hope to spring from my eyes
That the wraith I see would leave on its own
And then it throws the talons above my head
As I try to defend the shadows thrown

Jumping off a cliff
With my heart on my tongue
Beating hard with each moment
All prisoners hung

# Just Like That

And then just like that I forget everything
And i look at your picture staring
Thinking of all the things I wanna tell you about
All the mistakes n joys, all stories cowardly and daring

The things that brought me joy today
And the scoundrels that made me weep
All had a cure in our place
Some saccharine, some bittersweet

And then just like that
The foreboding storms didn't matter in the pin drop calm
Just as I stare at your face
I forget my bleeding heart was once in your palm

My screeches are a distant memory
So unrelated, so ungrateful.
How dare they try to break this trance
This sweet melody with the dance so cruel

And so now I play with melancholy
Sitting alone with a pencil and a poem
All these moments sitting on my fingers
All so empty without you knowing about them.

# Your Smiles on My Face

I won't even blame you for this time
It's all on me and the veins I split
Drowning choking in my blood
When I wrote our fate on a golden page
And then I decided to burn it

Among lines on pages and the streets I ran
Until my eyes were red and lips turned blue
Never have l been so consistent
As I have been in missing you

I'll never be able to pull myself back
Or unhear the warning as it rang true
Won't ever be able to wear my smile
Because it only ever looked good on you

I must be the first girl among my ancestors
To become a doormat for a man
First to keep the spear and cup aside
And strike the sword to make sure the blood never ran

# I'll Forget You Too

A hundred festives wouldn't bring back
The sweet agony of you digging the knife further
Going through the Nook and cranny of my heart
Looking for something to scar, something to murder

And My feelings were a living brute
Shrieking, howling, tied to a chain
Then came you, with your shining sword
Had all the useless creatures slain

I'll miss us some nights
When I'm absolutely alone
I'll keep finding ways to get you back
Find something for you to Atone

And then we'll be back will we?
Like the other problems were in vain
I chop off my arm
Before it has the chance to call your name
What with me glorifying our story,
Just because it has you as the villain

Or maybe I'll find "the one"
I've spent forever denying the existence of
And then I won't remember our seconds
Remain happy with a cage of diamond and a golden Cuff

Or maybe I'll be forever miserable
As lonesome as a thought
Wandering these streets grey and blue
Looking for something I long forgot
And then, maybe, and just maybe, I'll forget you too

 # Tell me

Because talking to you is a dopamine rush
Has me waiting for another hit
Every other source of happiness just fades to black and
white
I develop a tolerance for every other stimuli

I can survive not talking to you when I'm not
When I am I need to Without a breath without a syllable
I need you in my vicinity just an inch afar
So I can stare at you without blinking
And calm myself as I've been
Remind myself of your presence there
And remind myself you're still here

If it isn't too much trouble I'd like to slice through your
cerebrum
Take to the ventures of its calamities
The doors it broke and the planes it bit
The need to understand you will claim me before I do it

Tell me your thoughts
Tell me your dreams
Tell me what made you what you are today
And what you wish didn't
Tell me what keeps you up at night
And what you thought the toddler said
Which clouds look like a castle to you
Tell me what your demons knew
Which parts of yourself you adore the most
And which ones you'd like to cut
So I can love them all the same
And love you more for telling me

You're a puzzle I can't help but solve
But maybe I should stop myself
For you're a mystery I can't wait to unfold
But maybe you're nothing without it

# What is Pain?

Fight a lion that is pain
Slice your hand a gruesome pink
Crossing wars that is pain
How dare you call this jumbled nuisance agony?

How can your pain possibly matter
When so many suffered before you
How dare you say you're hurt little girl?
Bursting your heart is only a virtue

Even if you say you're chest is bleeding now
So many before you did too
What about all the people who fought in wars?
Who took a knife to their chests
How could you say you're broken inside
When all your bones still need

I think you need a little bit more fixing
To make you rough and tough?
How else will you realize enemies all around
If you don't see them in your family first

Just a little mending here and there
Won't be too much trouble I'm sure
Some cuts here, some slashes there
You'll be good as new when the leaves mature
Well who else will they learn it from?
If they don't fight their own kin?
How will they know how high the armour must be
Unless they have to wear it around their family

Feelings wouldn't have mattered if you were hungry and
starving
Your privileges mean nothing to you
You nitpick problems to address
Your list of grievances is endless through

Make sure you have a child
Teach them our ways of life
Know that humans were meant to fall and stand
Make sure they too never learn peace

# No Comrade

Your lies sound so sweet when i mix it with my dreams

Which one of us won the war?
Whose pieces could be counted more?

If we pluck out the ribs and open the heart
Whose pulse do you think stopped before

How could you not bleed the same I did?
I stretched my withering swollen arm
To realise I had no comrade

# Now I Know

I didn't know the anatomy of heart when its torn apart
Never knew the mechanics of when the nerves stop
I used to touch your chest to find the rhythm beneath my
fingers
To have my outstretched palm shred its flesh with a flick

I used to wait with my hand extended
Unaware of how a heart truly breaks
You peaked unrestrained at my soul
And now I know

 # Beneath the Earth

I want to become one with the earth
I can feel the core pulling me to it
It calls my name a heavier sigh
A siren singing a white lullaby

My heart is etched so deep in it
My limbs are immovable
The droplets on my face make an ugly web
Before they reach the dirt

My palm tingles remembering your touch
Your scarred hand and handing out my heart
The feel of your body and weight in me
Was ever the gravity enough

Now that mercy is truly beyond my reach
I lay on the dirt sobbing my heart out
Begging for the pavement to swallow me whole
Before I beg the skies for it.

# My Comfort Faith

Religions that go unanswered
Raging of the gods I angered
For its your arms that I see calmness bathe
In the familiarity of my comfort faith

With my mortal soul chasing the breeze
Your flashing shadows running at ease
My devoted eyes they pursue
I believe in you like the fanatics do

They scream madwoman on the streets
When I chant our memories
As useless as the pain I killed
For they didn't know you like I did

I carry your whispers like a sermon
Through the maze and the heavy burden
Of being the only one who saw you
Before the bloody rains came through

I simmer through your devoted cult
Writing epics holy and just
My prayers burning along with days
Singing you're my comfort faith

# I'll Take It

Avoid my eyes as I stare at you
Face the wall when I come through
Stolen glances through the lecture halls
Paint my day a golden hue

Sunlight taints you a broken brown
Your laughter that would suit a crown
Your soft gaze on my unaware eyes
Deep enough for me to drown

Intelligent eyes telling a story
Guiding me in all your glory
Hardworking crinkle between the brows
And the unique smile that's just yours

# Villains

The transition of you
From my saviour to the monster under my bed
In the blink of an eye
Has even me trying to catch my breath

The villains would burn the world to the ground
for their love, they said
But then you came along
And decided to set me ablaze instead

They say go back to the roots
But the roots are rotten and shedding

I want to let it consume me
I want to break down
I want to let the pieces of me Tumble, sink and drown

My screeching, screaming, howling
Didn't as much move a hair
As quickly as my silence tore your ear drums
As quickly as you led your feelings bare



The Needle in My Vein

# My White Flag

I'm tired of keeping up the armour
Against your spears as they come through

I sink to the ground exhausted and bloody
And weep dreaming about a different time

When I could stand in front of your eyes bare
When I didn't have to work constantly to Think and speak
if I dare
This constant hate tires me out

I'm tired of fighting in this war
I'm waving the white flag

# Needle in My Veins

I thought this pain was of youth and glamour
Sickness of heartbreak and fresh out the slammer
"It's a part of life honey, don't be dramatic"
She was right, maybe small, but it was a diamond casket

I never thought it to be evermore

I thought my bloodied shirt was nothing to be appalled
Red buttons were a trend after all

Stabs on my stomach to feel the appetite
No don't choke right now, that's for later
Aah I vomited blood again, damn it, I need to stop
wearing white

I thought my mangled legs were for a short while,
I wondered what shape would they be chainless?

How my eyes would tilt without the nails atop
How would this torment leave me be when my hands
are free
I had a suspicion when it didn't stop

It was too late when I could finally hear

The water in my blood whispering to the ocean i was
drowning in
About my blind eyes that could always see
The bread that was choking me and the bread i would
always eat
The rotten wheat that I saw too late
And said "It'll leave me soon enough"
Just to realise it had a home in here
Merrier than the one I did

And then one day I tasted it,
And decided to rip the poison out free
They opened me up with a sickle in hand
And couldn't tell it apart from me

www.ingramcontent.com/pod-product-compliance
Lightning Source LLC
Chambersburg PA
CBHW031809150726
47989CB00006B/2935